I'VE MADE MY PEACE... SO CAN YOU

A True Story of Metanoia: a conversion – a profound, spiritual conversion.

By

DEACON JIM BLANCHETTE

Published by Parker Publishers

Interior Design by Silvestra Z. Griffin

First Edition

I dedicate this book to God, the Author of redemption and the Giver of every grace, and to Our Lady of San Juan del Valle, whose maternal intercession obtained the mercies that made this possible.

Acknowledgment

I am deeply grateful to my grandmother, Mary, who first nurtured my faith when I was a child and planted seeds that would one day bear fruit. To my wife, whose patience truly reflects the heart of a saint — thank you for never giving up on me.

My sincere thanks to Father Greg T. Labus, who generously received my three-hour confession on that grace-filled day, which marked a turning point in my life.

I am also thankful to those who helped bring this book to life: my daughter, Amy; my good friend, Jennie, and her daughter, Hannah; and my neighbor, Bob, whose steady guidance supported me throughout the writing process.

I am especially grateful for my son's hockey career, which God used in an unexpected way to lead me more deeply into His grace.

I did not write this book out of self pity or to seek sympathy for my childhood. I wrote it for the young soul — and for the adults who once were those children — growing up amid alcoholism, substance abuse, or violence, so they may know they are seen, deeply loved, and never abandoned. My hope is that these pages remind them that even in the darkest rooms, God's light can enter and their pain does not have the final word. I pray that He softens even the hardest hearts, especially those worn down by years of dysfunction, and restores what has been wounded.

Table of Contents

Introduction

Metanoia[1] may sound like a theological term for scholars and saints, but I know it as something deeply personal—because I lived it. If you had told me twenty years ago that I would one day serve as a Deacon in the Catholic Church, I would have laughed—and probably given you a list of a hundred reasons why that could never happen. My life was not headed toward the altar. In fact, for a long time, it was moving in the opposite direction.

I grew up in a home marked by pain and brokenness. By my teenage years, I was chasing belonging in all the wrong places, through gangs, bad choices, and a lifestyle far from God. Even after marrying Barbara, the love of my life, and raising our children, faith was something I kept at a distance. My moral life as a police officer certainly didn't reflect the values I now hold dear.

But God has a way of writing the most unexpected stories, and sometimes He uses the moments we least expect

---

[1] **Metanoia**
Metanoia literally means repentance or penance. The term is regularly used in the Greek New Testament, especially in the Gospels and the Apostles' preaching. Repentance is demonstrated by faith, confessing sins, and producing fruits worthy of penance. It means a change of heart from sin to the practice of virtue. Conversion is fundamental to the teachings of Christ, was the first thing Peter demanded on Pentecost, and is considered essential to the pursuit of Christian perfection.
Hardon, J. A. (1980). *Modern catholic dictionary*. Doubleday.

to change everything. For me, it was a trip to Texas in 2006, a detour to a basilica I didn't even know existed, and an encounter with the Blessed Mother that would set my life on a completely different course.

This is the story of that journey, from rebellion to redemption, from skepticism to service. It's a story about grace, forgiveness, and the sometimes-humbling, often-surprising ways God works in our lives. It's also a deeply personal testimony about the beauty of the Catholic faith, the power of the sacraments, and the joy of answering a call you never thought you'd receive.

If you've ever doubted that God can reach into your life and change it—no matter where you've been—I hope that what you read here will assure you: He can. And He will. All you have to do is turn around and take that first step.

My path to the ministry of the diaconate was anything but predictable, which is precisely what makes it miraculous. And at the heart of it all was the Blessed Mother.

I grew up in a home overshadowed by dysfunction and an abusive, alcoholic father. By the age of thirteen, I had already decided my escape plan: to enlist in the Marines as soon as I was old enough to get out. After receiving the Sacrament of Confirmation at fourteen, I walked away from the Church, showing up only on the occasional Christmas or Easter.

Searching for belonging, I joined a gang in high school and drifted into a life of bad choices. Football gave me camaraderie, but my life was far from faith-filled. Then, at sixteen, I met Barbara, the love of my life, while working at a summer job for children with disabilities. Suddenly, my escape plan didn't seem so appealing. I stayed close to her, attended college, and, by what I can only call providence, was accepted to the University of New Haven despite my poor grades.

At twenty-one, I graduated and became a Hartford police officer. My moral compass, however, wasn't pointing due north. Barbara and I married in the Catholic Church a year later, and though she and her parents ensured our children received the Sacraments, my own faith life remained distant and inconsistent.

Then came October 21, 2006, a date I will never forget. I was in Texas for my son's first professional hockey game. My marriage was unraveling, and my faith felt non-existent. The next morning, I considered making choices that would only deepen that brokenness, but a quiet voice inside urged me to turn around. I listened. The first sign I saw was for the Basilica of Our Lady of San Juan del Valle. I didn't know it then, but that detour would change everything.

That day marked the beginning of my *metanoia*—a Greek word meaning repentance or a profound change of heart. It's a word that sounds theological, but for me, it's deeply personal. God used that moment, and the Blessed Mother's intercession, to draw me back from the edge and set me on a new course, one that would reconcile my marriage, renew my faith, and eventually lead me to serve as a Deacon in the Catholic Church.

This is the story of that journey: from rebellion to redemption, from skepticism to service. It's a story about grace, forgiveness, and the sometimes-humbling, often-surprising ways God works in our lives. It's also a testament to the beauty of the Catholic faith, the power of the

Sacraments, and the joy of answering a call you never imagined was meant for you.

If you've ever doubted that God can reach into your life and change it, no matter where you've been, I hope that what you read here will assure you: He can. And He will. All you have to do is turn around and take that first step.

I

Faith on the Second Floor (A Grandmother's Prayers In A House Divided)

"I am reminded of your sincere faith, a faith that lived first in your grandmother…" — 2 Timothy 1:5

It began with faith handed down through a grandmother's quiet witness. In a home shadowed by conflict, her prayers became my shelter and compass. This seed of faith, planted on the second floor, carried to Saint Joseph's Church, watered at Christmas Eve Midnight Mass, took root and began my journey toward God.

I was born in 1960 and raised in New Britain, Connecticut, the youngest of six children. My paternal grandparents lived on the second floor of our two-family home. My grandmother taught me how to pray. She was not only my spiritual guide but also a guardian angel, attempting to shield me from the constant domestic violence between my parents. My paternal grandfather passed away when I was six years old, but my memories of him are only good ones. I looked forward to walking with him to the corner as he headed to work as a New Britain police officer. My admiration for him greatly influenced my later decision to serve as a police officer myself.

In the 1960s, perhaps our culture did not view involvement in family matters the way it does today. Maybe my grandparents sought to compensate in other ways, by helping me learn to pray and encouraging me to spend as much time with them as possible.

As a child, I attended Mass weekly with my grandmother at Saint Joseph's in New Britain, where I received my Sacraments and attended CCD (Confraternity of Christian Doctrine). CCD provided me with a foundation in Catholic teaching and helped me grow in faith and understanding.

Every Christmas, my parents, siblings, and I attended Midnight Mass. When my grandmother passed away when I was twelve, I continued going to Mass on weekends. I sometimes felt extra motivation to attend, especially when I noticed that skipping Mass seemed to lead to injuries on the football field.

I once hoped to become an altar server. My mother deferred the decision to my father, and weeks passed without an answer. When I asked again, my mother told me my father had denied the request, saying I was too busy with sports and my newspaper route. I remember feeling profoundly disappointed, but I never questioned him; fear of his temper kept me silent. Like many adolescents, after Confirmation, I drifted away from regular Mass and confession.

Looking back, the clearest thread through my life is the one my grandmother stitched early: prayer as protection, presence, and purpose. Even when fear kept me from speaking up, and even when life after Confirmation pulled me away from church, that early formation stayed with me. It shaped my reverence for service in my grandfather's example, my longing for the altar, and my instinct to turn to God in hardship.

What began as a child's hands folded beside a grandmother became a steady, if sometimes quiet, path back to grace. The Church calls this *traditio fidei*, the handing on of faith. My life bears it out: in a turbulent home, God still worked through family, worship, and conscience to keep me, guide me, and call me forward.

Reflection Questions

1. Who in your life has quietly handed faith down to you, and how has their influence shaped your journey?

2. In seasons when you drifted from regular worship or prayer, what anchors—habits, people, or memories—helped lead you back?

3. How might God be calling you now to be a bearer of *traditio fidei* for someone else, even in small and unseen ways?

II

The Star I Wished On (And The Lies I Believed About Myself)

"I praise you, for I am fearfully and wonderfully made. Wonderful are your works; my soul knows it very well." —
Psalm 139:14

When I look back now, I wish I had truly believed these words as a child. At twelve years old, I didn't see myself as "wonderfully made." Instead, I let the voices of others convince me I was ugly. Those words sank deep into my heart, shaping how I saw myself, how I walked, and even how I held my head. Yet, even in that darkness, God was still there, sometimes as quietly as a bright star overhead during my early morning paper route, reminding me that He saw me differently.

There was nobody during my childhood—other than my grandfather in my early years—whom I viewed as a role model. He had a calm strength about him, the kind that didn't need to raise its voice to be respected. When I was with him, I felt steady, safe, and accepted. But when he was gone, that sense of safety disappeared. Without him, I didn't have anyone who made me believe I was worth something.

During those years, I often wondered why some boys seemed to have it all—confidence, charm, the easy way of fitting in wherever they went. I tried to act like them, thinking that if I walked or talked a certain way, maybe I'd be seen differently. But the comparison just made the loneliness sharper. I didn't know then that what I was really searching for wasn't approval—it was belonging.

Around that time, even some family members told me I was ugly. I believed it so deeply that I would spend hours wishing it weren't true. I delivered the morning edition of the *Hartford Courant*, which meant getting up before sunrise. I remember walking from house to house under a sky still scattered with stars. There was one star that always seemed brightest, straight overhead. I'd hum the tune from *Pinocchio*, *When You Wish Upon a Star*, and quietly make my own wish—to wake up one day and not hate the way I looked.

"Like a bolt out of the blue, faith steps in and sees you through; when you wish upon a star, your dreams come true."

As I got older, I turned to sports to build confidence. On the field, I could lose myself in motion, feel strong, and silence the noise in my head. For a little while, I wasn't the kid who was called names or looked down on—I was someone who could compete, someone who mattered. But even that confidence only lasted as long as the game did. When the whistle blew, the doubt came rushing back.

Eventually, I found my way into a group called Omega—a gang of kids who, like me, were looking for somewhere to belong. It started out feeling like family. We watched each other's backs and filled the void that home couldn't. But that search for acceptance came with a price. I started drinking, selling drugs, and pretending to be tougher than I really was. Deep down, I knew it wasn't who I was meant to be, but at least there, no one called me names. What I didn't have was anyone—teacher, coach, or friend—who helped me see myself through a different lens. There was no one to tell me that my value didn't depend on what others thought.

On my walks home from school, things weren't any easier. Some kids on a passing bus used to yell "Eeyore" out the window as they drove by. Eeyore—the gloomy donkey from *Winnie the Pooh*—hung his head low and spoke with a sigh. To me, it was proof that everyone saw what I felt inside. They didn't know that the way I walked, with my head down and shoulders slumped, was how I tried to protect myself. If I didn't make eye contact, maybe no one would notice me long enough to hurt me.

Years later, I ran into those same kids and asked why they called me that. They said they thought it was cute that I walked like the character Eeyore on Winnie the Pooh, with his head down all the time and just shuffling along. They had no idea how much those words had cut.

You might wonder if I ever thought about ending my life. I thank God that I didn't. But I know too many others who have. Words can wound deeply, and when a young person doesn't have someone to counter those lies with love, the pain can become unbearable. That's why I believe so strongly that we must protect and encourage our youth—to speak life into them before the world teaches them to doubt their own reflection.

Numerous studies show that negative words in childhood do far more than sting in the moment—they can change the way a child's brain processes self-worth and connection. Research indicates that exposure to verbal abuse is linked to changes in brain structure and function, particularly in areas that regulate emotion and self-perception.[1] One review found that harsh or humiliating language over time can blunt the brain's ability to respond to positive feedback, making it harder for a child to accept encouragement.[2] Another large-scale study estimated that more than **40 percent of children** have experienced verbal abuse at home—making it one of the most common and least recognized forms of maltreatment.[3]

What that means is that the childhood voice saying, *"You're not good enough,"* doesn't just bruise the heart—it reshapes how the mind expects to be treated. I didn't need research to prove it; I had lived it. But I also learned that kind words, spoken consistently and with love, have the power to rewire a wounded heart—to rebuild connection pathways, strengthen resilience, and restore dignity.

It took me years to realize that the harsh words of others never defined me. God's truth had been there all along: I was created in His image, and no insult or failure could erase that. Even when I went down the wrong path, He never stopped pursuing me. The voices of others told me I wasn't enough, but God's voice said, *You are mine.*

Today, I carry that truth with me. Every child—and every grown person still healing from their own childhood wounds—deserves to know that they are loved, valued, and wonderfully made. And as God's people, we are called to make sure that truth is spoken loudly enough to drown out the lies of the past.[234]

Reflection Questions

1. Have there been words spoken over you—whether in childhood or adulthood—that shaped how you saw yourself? How do they compare to what God says about you in His Word?

2. Who in your life might need to be reminded right now that they are "fearfully and wonderfully made"? How can you speak that truth to them?

3. In what ways can you be a voice of encouragement and protection for God's children in your community, especially those who may be silently carrying the wounds of bullying?

---

[2] Teicher, M. H., Samson, J. A., Sheu, Y. S., Polcari, A., & McGreenery, C. E. (2010). *Exposure to Parental Verbal Abuse is Associated with Increased Gray Matter Volume in Superior Temporal Gyrus. Neuroimage,* 49(1), 2801–2811.

[3] McCrory, E. J., & Viding, E. (2016). The Enduring Neurobiological Effects of Childhood Abuse and Neglect. Translational Psychiatry, 6(4), e799.

[4] UCL Institute of Cognitive Neuroscience. (2025, April). The Neuroscience of Childhood Verbal Abuse: Why We Need to Prevent It. Retrieved from ucl.ac.uk.

III

Behind Closed Doors
(Growing up in the shadow of
addiction)

"The Lord is close to the brokenhearted and saves those who are crushed in spirit." — Psalm 34:18

When I think about my childhood, these words speak directly to the reality I lived. Ours was not a safe or peaceful home—my father's drinking and violence cast a long shadow over our family. I didn't know it then, but the Lord was near, even in the moments when fear was thick in the air, when I was hit, or when my mother bore the marks of abuse. God's closeness wasn't always something I could feel, but looking back, I can see it—in the escapes to my aunt and uncle's home, the safe refuge of my godparents, and the quiet ways my mother tried to shield us from the worst of it.

Our home had a certain heaviness to it, a tension that clung to the air like humidity before a storm. Even as a child, I could sense it. The smell of whiskey mixed with cigarette smoke would signal the start of another bad night. The creak of the floorboards could make my stomach twist into knots because I never knew which version of my father was coming toward us—sleepy and quiet, or enraged and dangerous. We learned to read every sound, every movement, every change in his voice as if our safety depended on it—because it did.

My father was an abusive alcoholic who drank whiskey from the moment he awoke until he passed out. He worked sporadically as a union electrician, and when he drank, violence and verbal abuse were never far behind. Oddly enough, when he stopped drinking for a week or two, he often became even nastier. My mother would sometimes tell him he should start drinking again—at least then, she said, he'd be happy for a short while. Her words confused me back then, but I understand them now: she was simply trying to survive in a world where there were no good options.

Although my older brother bore the brunt of the hits, I will never forget the day I received mine. I don't know what I said to enrage him, but I remember the fear that took over my body as I ran for my bedroom. My heart pounded so loud I could hear it in my ears. I had just reached the doorway when he struck me from behind. The world spun as I flew across the room and landed hard on my bed. My body stung, but what hurt more was seeing my mother frozen in the hallway, eyes wide with terror. She did nothing—perhaps out of fear that stepping in would only make things worse. She herself suffered broken ribs, a broken arm, and black eyes over the years. Even as a little boy, I knew silence was her armor.

One night, my father was in a violent tirade. My mother locked us in the bathroom with her as he tried to break down the door. I can still hear the pounding—the sound of the wood splintering under his fists—and my mother whispering for us to be quiet. My brother's arm was around me, and I remember the cold tile floor under my bare feet, the smell of my mother's Jean Naté fragrance mixing with fear and sweat. When she finally opened the window and told us to climb out, the rush of cold air on my face felt like freedom. We ran to my godparents' house next door. No one called the police—that wasn't what people did in the 1960s. Divorce carried its own stigma, and I believe my mother chose enduring abuse over the judgment she feared as a divorced woman.

At times, she found other ways to protect us, sending us to stay with relatives for weeks or months. I spent time with my Aunt Julie and Uncle Frank in New York when I was three or four, and my siblings often stayed with aunts and uncles in Pennsylvania. At the time, I thought these trips were simply visits. Only later did I realize they were acts of protection. My aunt's house always smelled of tomato sauce and fresh laundry. It was warm, predictable, and safe. For a few days at a time, I could breathe without fear.

In that environment, survival meant learning to keep my mouth shut and speak softly. We walked on eggshells, constantly measuring our words. If we ever referred to my mother as "she" in my father's presence, we had better duck—because his temper would explode. My brother took up track; perhaps running was both a sport and a survival skill. I, on the other hand, learned to disappear in plain sight—to blend in, to make myself small, to become the kind of child who didn't cause waves.

Another coping mechanism was shutting people out when they disappointed me. If someone promised something and didn't follow through, I would cut them out completely. I felt alone in my feelings, convinced that relying on others only led to disappointment. I built walls and let only a few people inside, always on guard, always ready to push them away at the first sign of betrayal. Years later, Al-Anon meetings helped me understand that this pattern is common among children of alcoholics. Back then, I just thought it meant I was strong.

Growing up that way made me careful, quiet, and guarded, but it also made me resilient. I developed a deep sensitivity to others' moods and emotions, a kind of radar that has followed me into adulthood. I can walk into a room and feel the tension before anyone speaks. That skill, born out of survival, has shaped who I am—but so has the healing that came after. Over time, God has been patient with me, teaching me to trust again, to open the door for relationships, and to believe that not everyone will harm me.

Even in the locked bathroom, in the summers spent far from home, and in my self-imposed silence, I was never truly alone. The same God who promises to be close to the brokenhearted was there all along—waiting for the day I would let Him begin to heal what had been wounded for so long.

Reflection Questions

1. Looking back on painful seasons, where can you now see signs of God's protection, even if you didn't feel His presence at the time?

2. What "walls" have you built for survival that God might now be inviting you to take down gently?

3. How can your story of endurance and God's nearness encourage or comfort someone who feels brokenhearted today?

IV

Love That Changed My Escape Plan

(And showed me a different kind of home)

"For I know the plans I have for you, declares the Lord, plans for welfare and not for evil, to give you a future and a hope." — Jeremiah 29:11

In 1976, I thought I had my plan all figured out: graduate high school and get as far away from home as possible. But God had other plans—plans that began the summer I met Barbara.

We met while working at a summer job assisting adolescents with special needs. Barbara's mother was one of the association's founders, and her brother, who had special needs, attended the program. From the very beginning, Barbara and her family were a saving grace. They gave me something I had never known before: stability, normalcy, and a glimpse of what a loving home could look like.

Barbara's home life was the complete opposite of mine. In her family, kindness, calm, and respect were the norm—like the families I'd only ever seen on television in the 1960s. In my family, chaos reigned. Fighting, swearing, excessive drinking—it was the backdrop to nearly every gathering.

One example stands out. At my sister Denise's high school graduation party, my father, drunk as usual, picked a fight after Denise talked back to him—a boldness none of the rest of us shared. My mother told Barbara to run and hide at my godparents' house next door. Moments later, my father was chasing Denise down the street. The police arrived, but no arrests were made. True to the times, they told us to "keep the noise down" and deal with family matters privately. I once asked Barbara why she stayed with me despite all the drama. She smiled and said she found it entertaining. If reality television had existed then, we would have been a hit.

Before Barbara, my only escape plan was the Marines. I had a huge Marine sticker on my bedroom door and posters covering the walls. But meeting her shifted my direction. I decided to attend college and play football—something I'd never planned and certainly hadn't prepared for academically. None of my siblings had gone to college, and I had no idea how important the SAT (Scholastic Aptitude Test) was. I took it one morning before a football game, rushing through so I wouldn't be late. The highest score possible was 1500; I earned a 700—the bare minimum to get accepted into college. Looking back, I can see God's hand even in that, opening a door I hadn't even thought to knock on.

Meeting Barbara changed the course of my life. Without her, I would have chased my escape into the Marines. With her, I began to see the possibility of a different life—a life where home wasn't a battlefield. Even when my family's dysfunction spilled over into her world, she stayed. At one point in that early stretch, one of my closest friends convinced me to break up with Barbara. I listened to him, and the breakup lasted about a day. Within twenty-four hours, I knew I had made a huge mistake. She was the only real sense of stability I had in my life, the only person who showed me what normal felt like. Even back then, I didn't worry that she would leave me. The way she expressed herself, the way she cared, gave me confidence I didn't have anywhere else. I didn't trust many people during those years, but somehow, I trusted her. She was the exception.

Honestly, I don't know if it was love, faith, or her sense of humor that kept her around (probably all three). Now I see that what I thought was a coincidence was God's providence. His fingerprints were all over those years—from Barbara's steady presence to the unexpected path to college. He was guiding me toward a future and a hope I never could have imagined for myself.

Reflection Questions

1. Can you think of a time when your own plans were unexpectedly changed—and in hindsight, you can see God's hand in it?

2. Who in your life has been a steady, God-given influence, helping you see a different way forward?

3. Where might God be inviting you right now to trust His plan, even if it's different from the one you've been holding onto?

V

Mac & Cheese, Loss, and God's Quiet Provision
(Perseverance through scarcity and grief)

"But those who hope in the Lord will renew their strength;
they will soar on wings like eagles;
they will run and not grow weary,
they will walk and not be faint." — Isaiah 40:31

When I stepped onto the University of New Haven campus in 1978, I had no idea how much grit, humility, and faith it would take to make it to graduation. My acceptance likely had more to do with football than academics, but God was already setting the stage for me to learn resilience. That lesson began in my very first English class—when my essay became a public example of *how not to write.*

It happened on the first day of class. The professor, on sabbatical from Syracuse University, gave us a simple-sounding assignment: write an essay on a topic of our choice before the end of class. The following week, she began by saying, "I'm going to read one of the essays turned in last week. I won't say the student's name, because this is an example of how *not* to write an essay." She then read my essay in its entirety. She didn't need to say my name—my scarlet-red face gave me away.

When she finished reading my essay, it felt like my legs were knocked out from under me. The humiliation wasn't just about bad writing. It hit an old wound. Growing up, I had been criticized so often and so harshly by my father that I rarely believed I could do anything right. For a moment, sitting in that classroom, it felt like all those voices from my childhood had followed me to college.

I remember walking out and sitting in my car for over an hour, replaying every word she read. Part of me wanted to quit right then and drive home. But another part of me refused to give up. Even though I rarely received praise growing up, I always had this inner drive to do well. I never knew where it came from. Maybe it was because I watched Denise take college prep courses in high school, and something in me wanted to keep up. Maybe it was being the youngest and always feeling like I had something to prove.

Whatever it was, that drive showed up that day. I chose to stay—not for myself at first, but out of love for Barbara.

My faculty advisor recommended a tutor, and the school provided one for free. I worked with that tutor the entire semester and finished with a B in the class. During my freshman year, football helped cover most of my tuition through grants and work-study. But at the end of that year, I decided to quit the team and focus on academics—a decision that proved costly. The aid tied to football vanished, and my financial need grew.

At the same time, my parents sold our house and moved to Wyoming. I suddenly had no home to return to. Before college, I had worked for a realty company where my oldest sister's ex-fiancé held a management role. When I told him my situation, he offered me a job and an apartment in New Britain, Connecticut, 35 miles from campus. The building was crawling with cockroaches and mice, and I was living on food stamps and five-for-a-dollar boxes of macaroni and cheese.

Every Sunday, I ate dinner at Barbara's parents' home. To me, it was a banquet. After a year in that apartment, I pleaded for a move and was relocated to a better place in Middletown. A year later, my sister and brother-in-law bought a three-family home and let me live there in exchange for caring for the property.

Academically, things turned around. I made the Dean's List every semester through graduation in 1982, and I earned straight A's in one semester. But my college years were also marked by tragedy. In 1980, my sister Denise was killed in a car accident. She had escaped the violent home we grew up in, but her boyfriend—driving intoxicated—crashed. He survived, was acquitted of negligent homicide, but turned to heroin soon after and died of an overdose.

During that time, I also worked the midnight shift as an orderly at the same hospital where Denise worked with quadriplegic and paraplegic patients. She's the one who helped me get the job. When the accident happened, I had just finished a shift.

Her death shook our family in a way we never recovered from. My faith was barely there at the time, so I didn't wrestle with God the way some people do after tragedy. But

I did wrestle with the sadness of knowing she never found the kind of steady, healthy love I found with Barbara. She wanted stability so badly that she reached for the wrong person.

One memory of my sister has stayed with me for decades. When we were younger teenagers, she once told me she didn't think she would live a long life. She also told me that I would "be something someday." I had no idea what she meant at the time, but those words have followed me through life. Sometimes I wonder if she saw something I had not seen in myself.

During these years, I also learned perseverance when I was humiliated in class, resourcefulness when I was nearly homeless, and the sustaining grace of accepting help from a tutor and from Barbara's family. I learned that tragedy can find us even after we've left hard places, but that hope in the Lord truly can renew strength. Looking back, I see that those years weren't just about earning a degree—they were about learning to keep walking, even in grief, until God gave me the strength to soar.

Reflection Questions

1. When have you faced a moment where quitting felt easier than continuing—and what gave you the strength to press on?

2. Who has God placed in your life to help you keep going when your own resources feel insufficient?

3. What challenge or hardship in your past can now serve as a testimony of God's faithfulness to renew your strength?

VI

Faith on the Back Burner (Family, loss, and a sign I didn't expect)

"I do believe; help my unbelief!" — Mark 9:24

When Barbara and I married, and our daughter and son were born, we gave them the foundation of baptism and the sacraments. But if I'm honest, I had drifted far from regular Mass attendance. I was what some call a "C & E" Catholic—showing up on Christmas and Easter, sometimes. My leadership set the tone for our family, and instead of guiding them toward faith, I let it slide. I didn't reject God outright, but belief had become background noise in my life, present but quiet, easy to ignore.

Barbara had been raised in the Catholic faith and had received her sacraments of Baptism, First Holy Communion, and Confirmation. Our children followed the same path for the Sacraments. But our family's actual practice of the faith reflected my own habits. I led by example, and unfortunately, my example was one of sporadic church attendance and a casual relationship with God. I don't fault Barbara for not taking the kids regularly—she was following her husband's lead. Looking back, I see it was my responsibility to guide us toward God, and I failed in that.

Six years after our marriage, my mother passed away. That morning, I visited her in the hospital. She was intubated but conscious and tried to communicate with me using sign language—a skill our family had learned when my sister Renee's daughter was born deaf. Her hands moved the same message over and over, but my rusty skills failed me. I didn't understand. Eventually, she gave up, slipped into a coma, and my siblings began to arrive.

When my sister Renee came, I signed the movements our mother had made earlier. My sister interpreted them: "I'm going to die today." And she was right.

Before leaving her room, I asked my mother for something deeply personal: "If there's anything after this life, give me a sign." My Confirmation name was Thomas—chosen because I, too, wrestled with doubt. That night, after she passed, I woke suddenly. It was a warm night; I was sleeping in shorts with no blanket. Out of nowhere, I felt two cold hands rest on my legs. My wife was asleep beside me. The touch lingered, then was gone.

It startled me—but it wasn't enough to draw me back to the Church. The truth is, God was reaching out, even in my uncertainty. He was giving me a glimpse that He hears the prayers we're not even sure we believe in. But at the time, I wasn't ready to follow where He was leading—at least, not yet.

Reflection Questions

1. Have you ever prayed a hesitant prayer—one that was half-belief, half-doubt—and later realized God had answered it?

2. How has your spiritual leadership (or lack of it) shaped the faith life of those closest to you?

3. Where might God be reaching out to you right now, even if you feel you're not ready to follow?

VII

Holding the Line Without a Compass
(Faith absent in the fight of my life)

"Trust in the Lord with all your heart, and do not lean on your own understanding." — Proverbs 3:5

When I joined the Hartford Police Department in 1982, I was committed to enforcing the law, but not to living my faith. Aside from marrying Barbara in the Catholic Church that same year, I had little desire to attend Mass or seek God's direction. For years, I worked without a spiritual anchor, relying solely on my own instincts and judgment.

After several years on the job, I felt an unexpected pull—a desire to have the Catholic chaplain ride along with me. Maybe God was trying to get through. But the Catholic chaplain was on an extended leave, and I was assigned the Methodist chaplain instead. I'm still not sure what prompted me to open up to him, but one night I spoke as if I were in a confessional, unburdening myself of guilt. His response stunned me: "Jim, it's okay. All you guys do it. Not a problem." I asked if he was condoning what I'd confessed, and he said yes.

Later, I learned that the same chaplain had been arrested and served prison time. That experience taught me how dangerous it can be when someone in a position of spiritual guidance distorts the truth—how easily lives can be steered off course. Still, I didn't turn back to my faith.

A couple of years before my mother passed away, she called me while I was on duty. My father had been drinking heavily and threatened to kill her. She didn't want to call the police, but I knew he had several guns in the house. When I arrived, I found him passed out on his bed. Standing over him, I had a dark thought: *just shoot him.* This was the man who had been physically abusive to my mother and us children for so long. I felt a surge of hatred I didn't know I was capable of. In the few seconds where the thought of pulling the trigger crossed my mind, years of memories flashed through me: my mother's bruises, her whispered apologies for his outbursts, the nights she hid in fear, and now the sight of her in a wheelchair while he threatened to shoot her. It all collided at once.

Part of me wanted to end it. Not out of revenge, but out of a desperate urge to stop the abuse she could no longer fight against, physically or mentally. For a moment, the uniform felt like power I'd never had growing up, power that could finally protect her. But at the same time, the uniform reminded me of something else—restraint, responsibility, and a duty not to deliver my own justice.

What ultimately stopped me wasn't the badge. It was my family. I had Barbara, and we had our first daughter by then.

The life I had worked so hard to build flashed before me, and I knew I couldn't throw it all away. I also knew that killing him wouldn't free my mother. She was locked in what I would later understand as a trauma bond. Even after I brought her to live with us for a short time, she returned to him within a month.

That night shaped the rest of my police career. I became hypersensitive to domestic violence calls. I had zero tolerance for men who harmed women and children. I knew too well the damage it inflicted. I responded to those scenes with a firm hand and a clear message: the cycle of abuse ends here.

That moment with my father could have destroyed everything. Instead, it revealed that even in the darkest corner of my life, when my moral compass was clouded, something in me still knew where the line was.

The job brought other personal trials. Shortly before retiring, I was the arresting officer in an incident involving my own nephew. His mother—my oldest sister—believed his story and persuaded my other siblings and their spouses to take his side. They didn't speak to me for five years.

By the time I retired in 2002, as a lieutenant, my career looked admirable from the outside. I'd earned commendations, including the medal of valor, for choosing not to use deadly force when a gunman fired three shots past my face during a close combat struggle. But inside, I was carrying unspoken trauma. Flashbacks were real, though I never sought counseling—the stigma was too strong. Like many officers, I coped through unhealthy means: drinking with colleagues, swapping dark humor about the night's calls.

I saw too many marriages around me crumble under the weight of the job. I knew mine could be next. The truth is, I had been holding the line as a police officer, but I was drifting as a man—confusing survival for success and leaning entirely on my own understanding rather than on the Lord who could truly steady my steps.

Reflection Questions

1. Have you ever followed someone's advice, only to realize later it had led you further from God's truth? How did you respond?

2. In what areas of your life are you most tempted to "lean on your own understanding" rather than trust the Lord?

3. How might you invite God to be your anchor in places where the demands or pressures of life have pulled you away from Him?

VIII

The Detour I Didn't Plan
(When God redirected my steps)

"In their hearts humans plan their course, but the Lord establishes their steps." — Proverbs 16:9

In 2006, our son signed with a minor league hockey team in Rio Grande Valley, Texas—the Killer Bees. I promised him I'd be there for his first game. Barbara didn't join me on the trip; our marriage was strained, mostly because of my own choices.

The truth is, Barbara not being on that trip said more about our marriage than I wanted to admit. Years of emotional detachment had gotten between us. Children of alcoholics learn early how to shut people out, even the ones they love, and I had been doing that to her for years. As my career advanced and life felt more stable, I convinced myself I didn't need her as much. I didn't miss her on that trip—at least not in a way I could feel then. What I felt was distance, a kind of numbness that had seeped into our marriage long before I ever boarded the plane. Looking back, I see that I wasn't just disconnected from Barbara. I was disconnected from myself. My faith life was nonexistent.

When I arrived in Texas, my intentions for the weekend were far from spiritual. At a traffic light near my hotel, I noticed a sign: *World's Greatest Strip Club*. I even checked my watch to see if I had time to stop before the game. I didn't. After the game, I considered going, but it was closed. The next morning, I tried again—but they wouldn't open until later. Disappointed, I decided to drive around and sightsee.

That's when I saw another sign: *Mexico – 2 miles*. As I approached the border, I hesitated. Over the years, I had learned how to detach from everything: trauma, emotions, even the people who care about me. A clinical social worker, who was a co-worker told me I coped by laughing at things that weren't funny, a defense that had started during my police career without me even realizing it. But in that moment at the border, the detachment broke.

There was a clear inner voice that said, "No. Don't go. You're not coming back." It wasn't dramatic, but it was firm. And I didn't take it as a metaphor. I believed it. I felt it in my body. Something told me that crossing that line, literally and figuratively, would take me somewhere I wouldn't return from. I turned the car around as fast as I could, not out of logic but out of instinct, fear, and maybe the smallest spark of grace.

As I turned around, my eyes landed on a different sign: *Basilica of Our Lady of San Juan del Valle*. For years, I avoided telling the full truth about what led me to the shrine in Texas that day. I hinted at it. I spoke around it. I even preached a third-person version of it during a televised Mass, not naming myself, but describing "a man" whose life had been turned upside down by grace. When I got home, my wife wasn't thrilled that I had shared it publicly. But I told her what I knew in my heart: this part of the story matters.

There is nothing negative in telling the truth about what God did for me.

The truth is this: before my conversion in 2006, I had made a promise to God in a moment of fear, desperation, and clarity. And I had spent months pretending that promise didn't exist.

It happened at the Ice Box Café, my restaurant, long before the trip to Texas. One of my cousins, who worked with me, gave me marijuana that had been laced with something far stronger. Minutes later, I went into a full physical panic—my breath slipping in and out, my heart racing out of control, my body convinced it was dying. For three hours, I was on my knees, begging God to spare me.

I prayed, "If You get me out of this, I'll do whatever I have to do."

And then, like many do when the crisis passes, I went right back to my life. I didn't return to church. I didn't change anything. But that promise to God lodged itself somewhere deep inside me, even though I never spoke of it again.

Months later, when I was in Texas to watch my son play hockey, that forgotten promise resurfaced. Not gently, suddenly.

I had planned to go anywhere except toward God: the strip club I saw by my hotel, or Mexico, only a couple of miles away. But that memory is what made me turn the car around.

That is what brought me into the parking lot of the Basilica of Our Lady of San Juan del Valle. That is what put me on the path that changed everything.

When I stepped out of my car, the heat was brutal, and the wind was strong—twenty-five to thirty miles an hour. I walked toward the outdoor Stations of the Cross, starting accidentally at the wrong end. Before correcting myself, something caught my eye at the thirteenth station, the Pietà.

In the Blessed Mother's hand lay a rose petal.

A real one.

Not glued.

Not wedged.

Not moving in the wind that was nearly pushing me sideways.

I told myself it must be glued down. I even reached out to check, like a doubting Thomas. But when my fingers touched it, it lifted, loose and weightless. The wind didn't move it, but my hand did.

That moment stopped me. It softened something in me. It reminded me again of that promise I had made when I was on my knees at the café.

So, I walked the Stations of the Cross properly. And when I finished, before I went inside the Basilica, I called my Aunt Julie and Uncle Frank. They had spent years urging me to reconcile with my oldest sister. For five years, I refused. That day, unbeknownst to me, would be the start of a reconciliation in more ways than one.

Everything that followed—the call of the Blessed Mother, the moment of turning around at the border, the rose petal, the pull into that shrine—was rooted in that forgotten promise.

At the time, I didn't understand why I ended up at the Basilica instead of Mexico or the strip club. Now, I see it as one of the first quiet ways God began steering my steps—away from temptation and toward a place where my heart could start to be softened. It wasn't yet my full turning point, but it was the beginning of the road to my *metanoia*.

Reflection Questions

1. Can you recall a time when your plans took an unexpected turn, only to realize later that God had redirected you for a reason?

2. What "detours" might God be using right now to steer you away from harm and closer to Him?

3. How can you become more aware of God's small, quiet interventions in your daily life?

IX

Forty Years Since My Last Confession
(The day I came home)

"If we confess our sins, he is faithful and just to forgive us our sins and to cleanse us from all unrighteousness." — 1 John 1:9

Inside the Basilica, the first thing I noticed were dusty crutches, walkers, and canes leaning against the wall—evidence, perhaps, of prayers answered long ago. At first, I thought they might be props, but the years of dust told a different story.

The massive sanctuary could seat nearly 1,800 people, but only about ten were scattered in the pews. I sat toward the back, knelt, and prayed an *Our Father* and a *Hail Mary*. Leaning back, I closed my eyes. There was no music playing, no one speaking aloud—yet suddenly, I heard the sound of many voices praying. The words were inaudible, but the presence was unmistakable. I opened my eyes—everyone was silent. I closed them again, and the praying returned.

Then, without warning, an overwhelming desire to go to confession gripped me. I hadn't been in nearly forty years—probably just before my Confirmation—and for decades I'd dismissed it as a waste of time. I got up and walked to the back, where a middle-aged woman sat at an information booth. I asked if a priest was available. She pointed to a nearby door and told me not to knock, but to wait until the priest came out.

Five minutes passed. Then ten. Then thirty. The waiting became a battle: the devil in one ear whispering, *"Leave, this is pointless,"* and the angel in the other saying, *"Stay, don't go."* After forty-five minutes, the door opened, and Father Greg Labus stepped out.

I asked if he would hear my confession and told him it had been decades. He asked if I knew how to make a proper confession; I said yes. Still, he stepped away and returned with a sheet titled *Guide for Confession – Examination of Conscience Based on the Ten Commandments.* Under each commandment was a list of searching questions:

1. I am the Lord your God. You shall not have strange gods before me.

- Do I give God time every day in prayer?

- Do I seek to love Him with my whole heart?

- Have I been involved with superstitious practices, or have I been involved with the occult?

- Do I seek to surrender myself to God's word as taught by the Church?

- Have I ever received Communion in the state of mortal sin?

- Have I ever deliberately told a lie in Confession or withheld a mortal sin from the priest?

- Are there other "gods" in my life—money, security, people, etc.?

2. You shall not take the name of the Lord your God in vain.

- Have I used God's name lightly or carelessly?

- Have I been angry with God?

- Have I wished evil upon anyone?

- Have I insulted a sacred person or abused a sacred object?

3. Remember to keep holy the Lord's Day.

- Have I deliberately missed Mass on Sundays or Holy Days of Obligation?

- Have I tried to observe Sunday as a family day and a day of rest?

- Do I do needless work on Sunday?

4. Honor your father and your mother.

- Do I honor and obey my parents?

- Have I neglected my duties to my spouse and children?

- Have I given my family a good religious example?

- Do I try to bring peace into my daily life?

- Do I care for my aged and infirm relatives?

5. You shall not kill.

- Have I had an abortion, or encouraged or helped anyone to have one?

- Have I physically harmed or killed anyone?

- Have I abused alcohol or drugs?

- Have I given scandal, leading others into sin?

- Have I been angry or resentful?

- Have I harbored hatred in my heart?

- Have I mutilated myself through sterilization?

- Have I encouraged or condoned sterilization?

- Have I participated in or approved of euthanasia?

6. You shall not commit adultery.

- Have I been faithful to my marriage vows in thought and action?

- Have I engaged in any sexual activity outside of marriage?

- Have I used any method of contraception or artificial birth control in my marriage?

- Has each sexual act in my marriage been open to new life?

- Have I been guilty of masturbation?

- Do I seek to control my thoughts and imagination?

- Have I respected members of the opposite sex, or treated them as objects?

- Have I been guilty of homosexual activity?

- Do I seek chastity in thought, word, and action?

- Am I careful to dress modestly?

7. You shall not steal.

- Have I stolen what is not mine?

- Have I made restitution for what I have stolen?

- Do I waste time at work, school, or home?

- Do I gamble excessively, depriving my family of their needs?

- Do I pay my debts promptly?

- Do I share what I have with those in need?

- Have I cheated anyone out of what is justly theirs?

8. You shall not bear false witness against your neighbor.

- Have I lied or gossiped?

- Do I speak badly of others behind their backs?

- Am I sincere in my dealings with others?

- Am I critical, negative, or uncharitable in my thoughts about others?

- Do I keep confidential things private?

- Have I injured someone's reputation through slander?

9. You shall not desire your neighbor's wife.

- Have I consented to impure thoughts?

- Have I caused them through impure reading, movies, TV, conversation, or curiosity?

- Do I pray immediately to banish impure thoughts?

- Have I behaved inappropriately with members of the same or opposite sex?

10. You shall not desire your neighbor's goods.

- Am I jealous of what others have?

- Do I envy the families or possessions of others?

- Am I greedy or selfish?

- Are material possessions the purpose of my life?

Reflection Questions

1. When you think about your own life, which "commandment areas" are hardest for you to surrender to God?

2. How might an honest self-examination—before God and without excuses—bring you closer to His grace?

3. What keeps you from fully receiving God's forgiveness, and how can you release that today?

X

Two Miles from Mexico, Steps from Mercy
(The confession that changed everything)

"I will sprinkle clean water upon you, and you shall be clean from all your uncleanness; and from all your idols I will cleanse you. A new heart I will give you, and a new spirit I will put within you." — Ezekiel 36:25–26

As I read through the Ten Commandments Father Labus had given me, the reality hit hard: *Wow, I have a lot of confessing to do.* I told Father, "We have a big problem here, because it has been approximately forty years since my last confession." I asked him how much time he had, and he assured me, "All the time you need."

We walked into the room he had come from and sat down. About three hours passed as I poured out my life; I had laid bare decades of sin. I remembered my youth, when penances always seemed harsh—countless Our Fathers and Hail Mary's for not being nice to my siblings or disobeying my parents or grandparents. So, I braced myself, expecting a lifetime's worth of prayers as a crushing penance. Instead, Father absolved me of my sins and said, "Jim, for your penance, I want you to go and do something nice for someone." I almost fell off my chair. He must have noticed my shock because I was fully expecting to say prayers for the rest of my life. I felt relieved—until he added, "I want to see you at Mass tomorrow." It felt shockingly light—until I realized what God was really after wasn't punishment, but my heart.

The next day was Sunday. I recall looking at him with a hint of reluctance and replying, "Okay."

I walked out of the Basilica lighter, freer, forgiven. This was the heart of my *metanoia*—the moment my story turned from running from God to walking with Him. It wasn't the end of my journey, but it was the true beginning of coming home.

I fulfilled my penance by going to Walmart to buy groceries and a charcoal grill for my son and his roommates, who had told me they needed both. Looking back, I realized I could have fulfilled my penance by donating to someone or an organization in need, but at the time, this seemed like the right thing to do. After delivering the items, I returned to the hotel to rest before my son's evening game. My only questionable choice was stopping at a barbecue restaurant in a junkyard—a place my family will tell you was exactly my kind of spot. Unfortunately, the pulled pork and chicken dinner tasted off, and I only ate a small portion. Later that night, I paid the price.

My son's team won the game, and afterward we had dinner together before I returned to the hotel. I wasn't tempted by the strip club nearby—something that would have been a temptation in my past. I simply retired for the evening.

When morning came, I didn't even hesitate about going to Mass. I attended the morning service at Our Lady of San Juan del Valle and received the Eucharist from Father Labus, who smiled when he saw me.

That Sunday afternoon, I was scheduled to fly home. At the airport, I realized something strange—I wasn't afraid. Usually, I went straight to the bar for drinks to calm my nerves before a flight. This time, I had no desire for alcohol at all. I felt calm, peaceful, and steady.

The flight was uneventful. When I arrived home and walked through the door, Barbara was standing there. I saw her differently than I had in years—radiantly beautiful, not because she had changed, but because I had. The first words out of my mouth were, "I love you." She gave me a skeptical look and walked away. I understood her reaction—it had been years since I'd said those words sincerely—and I made it my mission to win back her trust and love.

Barbara would later tell you it took over a year and a half before she believed the change in me was real. She assumed it was just a phase. But from that moment, I was different.

I soon felt drawn to church and, for the first time in my life, began reading the Bible. The very first passage I opened to—by sheer chance—was Colossians 3:5–17, titled *Renunciation of Vice*:

"Put to death, then, the parts of you that are earthly: immorality, impurity, passion, evil desire, and the greed that is idolatry… And over all these put-on love, that is, the bond of perfection… And whatever you do, in word or deed, do everything in the name of the Lord Jesus, giving thanks to God the Father through him."

I didn't realize it at the time, but this passage would become a guide for my return to God.

Too often, we judge people by their past. If I had been judged by who I was before October 21, 2006, I doubt I would be a Catholic Deacon today. Many saints—Saint Augustine among them—lived far from holiness before their conversion. My oldest sister's favorite saint was Saint Monica, Augustine's mother, who prayed unceasingly for her son to turn from sin. I believe her prayers, and those of others, helped pave my way.

For a long time, I feared that people who knew the old me would confront me about my past. During a New Testament class, I watched a documentary that depicted Saint Paul being told, "I know who you are, and I know what you've done." Paul replied, "I've made my peace with the Lord my God." In that moment, my fear vanished.

Before my conversion, I was pro-abortion, pro–death penalty, and dismissive of the Sacrament of Reconciliation. After my metanoia, my beliefs aligned fully with the Church. Sins and behaviors I once embraced became appalling. I didn't lose the memory of my sins—my thorns in the flesh remind me daily of the contrast between life with God and life without Him. And life without God is hell.

That weekend in Texas became the hinge of my life. My metanoia began in that Basilica, but it was sealed in that confessional. Forty years in the wilderness had ended. I had come home.

Reflection Questions

1. Have you ever experienced God's mercy in a way that felt lighter than you expected, yet transformed you more deeply than you imagined?

2. What "old self" habits or beliefs might God be inviting you to put to death so He can give you a new heart and spirit?

3. How can you live out your "penance" today by showing tangible kindness to someone who may not expect it from you?

XI

When Hell Freezes Over (How God thawed years of silence)

"Be kind to one another, tenderhearted, forgiving one another, as God in Christ forgave you." — *Ephesians 4:32*

When I retired from the Hartford Police Department, I tried a handful of jobs, but none brought lasting satisfaction. In January 2006, I opened a small restaurant in Cromwell, Connecticut, called the Ice Box Café. By then, I was still estranged from my siblings. The rift—caused by my arrest of my nephew—had gone on for five years.

Then, on the Saturday before Easter of 2007, God arranged what I can only describe as a divine appointment with a touch of humor. I had stepped out to buy wine for Easter dinner at the local package store. There, standing in the aisle, was my brother Michael. We hadn't seen or spoken to each other in years. I didn't know what to expect—but he smiled, and we hugged. I told him about the café, and we went to see it together.

Before long, Michael began working with me. He worked behind the counter, helped with food prep and cooking, and took on whatever repairs or painting the café needed. One day, he suffered a medical emergency. Moments like that often have a way of bringing families back together, and this was no exception. Soon after, I saw my oldest sister. Without hesitation, I said, "If there was anything I did that hurt you, I'm sorry." That was the first crack in the wall that had separated us.

Reconciliation grew from there—so much so that my nephew, the same one I had arrested, later asked me to be the godfather to his son. I asked my sister if she had ever imagined that could happen. She laughed and said, "When hell freezes over." My nephew had another son during the radio silence with my siblings, who was born on my birthday. We often joked that our late mother must have been pulling strings from heaven. But in my heart, I knew it was God— quietly restoring what had been broken.

This was more than family reconciliation. It was one of the first clear signs of my *metanoia*—my turning back toward God. I didn't yet realize how much He was preparing me for the next chapters of my life, but I could sense He was beginning to write a very different kind of story in me.

Reflection Questions

1. Is there someone in your life with whom God might be prompting you to take the first step toward reconciliation?

2. How have you seen God use "chance" meetings or unexpected events to heal broken relationships?

3. What small act of humility—like an apology—might open the door for God to do a greater work of restoration in your life?

XII

Welcome Home
(Finding my way back to the Catholic Church)

"I rejoiced when they said to me, 'Let us go to the house of the Lord.'" — *Psalm 122:1*

After my conversion experience in Texas, I didn't run straight back into the Catholic Church. I began by visiting a few non-denominational Christian churches, invited by friends. The music was lively, the people were friendly, and in one place, they even served Starbucks coffee in the lobby. But as engaging as those services were, I couldn't shake the feeling that something was missing.

The first church I visited had plenty of music and energy, but very little Scripture. Everyone seemed genuinely happy—laughing, singing, and greeting each other warmly—but I felt no connection. I attended once and knew it wasn't where God was calling me. The second church met in a rented hall. Again, there was a lot of music, some Scripture, and smiling faces all around. But my heart still felt restless.

Finally, I called my oldest sister, a faithful Catholic who, along with her husband John, attended the Oratory of Jesus in New Britain, Connecticut. She put me in touch with Sister Teresa, who became an important guide in my return to the Church. Sister Teresa encouraged me to attend Mass at St. Joseph's Church in New Britain—the parish where I had grown up.

The moment I walked into St. Joseph's, the fragrance of incense greeted me. A warmth swept over me. I knew I was home. In the vestibule hung a painting of Jesus embracing a man in the clouds—"Welcome Home." It became one of my favorite images, perfectly capturing what I felt that day. When Mass ended, I was at peace and certain that the Catholic Church was where I belonged.

I began attending weekly Mass with my wife, my eldest sister, and her husband at Sacred Heart Church in East Berlin. Before long, my brother-in-law, a lector, invited me to serve as one too. Proclaiming the Word became a source of joy and growth for me, and the pastor offered guidance that deepened my understanding of Scripture and my role in worship.

Teaching CCD soon followed. Somehow, stepping into teaching felt natural, almost like slipping into a role I didn't know I'd been preparing for. I started by assisting with a second-grade class and later helped a friend with a Confirmation group. When the second-grade instructor struggled to teach the Ten Commandments, I realized how she was using the same rigid, joyless approach I had grown up with. That kind of teaching may check the boxes, but it doesn't reach the heart. I wanted the opposite for my students. When she asked me to cover a class, I found a video that made them simple and memorable for children. It worked, and I still use those same teaching techniques today.

From the beginning, my goal was simple: make the faith accessible, enjoyable, and grounded in the heart, not just the head. I would tell the kids the same thing I tell adults when I preach: "I'm not talking to you from my head. I'm talking from my heart and from my soul."

I've never been a theologian, and I still struggle to recall chapter-and-verse citations the way some can. I'm not the deacon who fires off Scripture quotes at dinner parties. What I can offer—what feels genuine to me—is a way of teaching that is simple, clear, and rooted in lived experience. It's why I often recommend *Catholicism for Dummies* to adults preparing for the sacraments. It makes the faith graspable rather than intimidating. It was also one of the first books I bought to relearn the basics of Catholicism. It was the perfect reintroduction—clear, approachable, and free of intimidation. Though I'd been raised Catholic, I had tuned out much of what I'd been taught as a child. This book helped fill in the gaps and answer the questions I might have been too embarrassed to ask.

That desire for clarity followed me into parish life. When I eventually took over our parish's religious education program, the first thing I did was replace the curriculum. The books they had been using were far too complex, even for the parents trying to help their children. I redesigned the program to be child-friendly, adult-friendly, and rooted in the basics. Faith formation shouldn't feel like trying to interpret a textbook. It should feel like coming home to something true and welcoming.

Teaching those children didn't just help them understand their faith. It helped me find my voice—simple, sincere, and grounded in the heart.

My love for God and the Catholic faith was growing quickly, and I wanted to learn more. At the Oratory, Father David led weekly presentations on different topics. One night, the topic was "Apologetics." I sat there wondering why he would dedicate an entire evening to teaching people how to apologize. It didn't take long to realize my mistake—Apologetics wasn't about saying "I'm sorry," it was about defending the faith. While I'll never be a theologian, I learned that my defense of the faith could come from my heart and my own lived experience, while also being grateful for those called to defend it intellectually.

Looking back, my *metanoia* wasn't just about turning away from my old life—it was about turning toward the fullness of faith I'd never fully embraced before. God hadn't simply called me back to church. He had called me home.

Reflection Questions

1. Have you ever searched for "home" in your faith life, only to realize it was closer than you thought?

2. What sights, sounds, or traditions make you feel most connected to God's presence in worship?

3. How might God be calling you not only to return to Him but also to serve others in His Church?

XIII

"If You Are Found Worthy"
(The long road to the Diaconate)

"Let us not grow weary in doing good, for in due season we will reap, if we do not give up." — Galatians 6:9

I cannot pinpoint the exact moment I felt called to the Diaconate. No one approached me about it. It wasn't a suggestion from a priest or a fellow parishioner—it was simply something I felt God quietly placing on my heart. At the time, I was attending daily Mass, serving as a lector, and deeply involved in parish life. My past experiences, my renewed faith, and my love for Scripture stirred a desire to serve in a deeper way.

Before my metanoia, I could not bear to hear Christmas music. It triggered painful memories of my father's drinking and violence on Christmas Eve. Alcoholism in our home didn't take a holiday—it was magnified. After my conversion, that changed. The joy of Christmas returned to me, and even my wife was surprised the first time we heard carols playing. She instinctively went to change the station, but I told her to leave it on. My heart had healed enough to welcome the songs again.

In 2008, I decided to apply to the Diaconate. The application packet included details on the duties, qualifications, and expectations for deacons. One particular guideline stood out: if a married deacon's wife passes away, he may never remarry. That did not trouble me in the least. In fact, reading it only strengthened my conviction that this calling was real.

At the orientation meeting, about forty men were present. The priest leading the session reiterated the remarriage rule right away. He explained that in the past, some men had gotten far into the process only to withdraw over that requirement. This time, he wanted to be clear from the start. Sure enough, as soon as he finished, about half the men stood up and left.

We were then given a baseline knowledge test—something they would compare to another test after years of formation. I remember one question I got wrong: *What are the Four Marks of the Church?* I know them now and will never forget them, but at the time, I was embarrassed by my answer.

The interview process followed soon after. I met with one priest and two deacons. The questions were fair, and I felt my answers reflected both my faith and my readiness. There was no indication that I had raised any concerns. I left confident I would be accepted.

That spring and summer, I waited eagerly for the letter. Every day, I went to the mailbox like a child expecting a special gift from a grandparent. In early August, it finally arrived. My heart sank as I read the word *deferred.* There were three possible outcomes: acceptance, deferral, or rejection. I had not been rejected outright, but I would have to wait two more years before reapplying.

I remember returning to the garden to pull weeds, stunned. I thought *I never expected this.* And then, in my head, I heard: *I didn't tell you it would be easy.* I stopped, looked up, and said aloud, "You're right. And I'm not going to quit."

Later, I asked our pastor if he knew why I had been deferred. He told me he had mentioned to the panel that I only received the Eucharist from clergy, and he thought that might indicate "a mental problem." I initially assumed he was joking, but he wasn't. I didn't find it funny.

God's sense of humor was at work in the meantime. In 2009, I learned that the Connecticut Department of Children and Families (DCF) was hiring social workers—and they were accepting candidates with criminal justice degrees. I applied and was hired in 2010. I wanted to help people in a hands-on way, and this was undoubtedly an opportunity to do so.

The work was nothing like my 20 years as a police officer. As I often put it, police work is "cuff them and stuff them," but social work is "love them and hug them." That doesn't mean there wasn't overlap—both roles required stabilizing crises, ensuring safety, and making referrals. But as a social worker, I was in the trenches with families for months at a time.

My own life experiences helped me connect with people in ways that surprised them—and me. In the beginning, there was often resistance when I showed up at the door. But when I noticed a rosary, a picture of Jesus, or an image of the Blessed Mother, I knew I had a starting point. Over time, many families didn't want me to close their cases because they felt heard and respected. One comment I heard repeatedly was, "Are you sure you're a social worker? You're too nice." That was both amusing and sad, because it revealed how low their expectations were.

When DCF launched a new initiative called *Partners in Change*, the idea was to treat families with respect, listen to them, and partner with them. I was shocked that this needed to be taught—I thought it was obvious. But one manager told me bluntly, "We've been training social workers to be mean to families for years." Sadly, I found that to be true in many cases. Resistance to the new program was strong, and the old ways persisted. A teenager once asked me, "Do you know what DCF stands for? Destroying Children and Families." It broke my heart that I often had to agree.

Halfway through my first year, I received notice that I was being laid off due to budget cuts. To my surprise, some of the parents I had worked with gave such positive feedback to a counseling agency that they wanted to hire me. Unfortunately, my lack of a social work or counseling degree made it impossible. However, the layoff was eventually rescinded, and I stayed for a decade.

I truly believe that without my faith in God, I would not have lasted in that role. I often told struggling coworkers to think of themselves as wearing the armor of God. Every Monday, you put it on; by Friday, it's dented and scratched. You need to repair it—through prayer and the sacraments— to be ready for battle again. I made every effort to attend daily Mass, either before work or during lunch.

Four years in, I was promoted to supervisor—an unpopular move for some, given my short tenure. Six months later, I was demoted. On Good Friday, a coworker asked why I had ashes on my forehead and what booklet I was holding. I told her it was a Lenten reflection booklet and let her look through it. Not long after, I was called to Human Resources and accused of handing out Scripture at work. My supervisor told me, "Check your faith at the door." I refused. To do so would have been hypocritical.

The rest of my DCF career was challenging. Supervisors seemed intent on finding fault. One even told me, "I can't believe you're still here. They're out to get you." When I asked if it was because of my faith, she said, "Absolutely."

Looking back, my first application's deferral was not a setback—it was preparation. Those years at DCF taught me resilience, compassion, and the cost of discipleship. They strengthened the very faith that first stirred my call to the Diaconate. My metanoia had moved me from simply returning to the Church to preparing my heart for a lifetime of service, no matter how long the road to ordination would be.

Reflection Questions

1. Have you ever experienced a delay or deferral in something you deeply felt called to do? How did you respond—did it weaken or strengthen your resolve?

2. In what ways has God used unexpected detours to prepare you for future service or leadership?

3. How does your faith sustain you when facing hostility, misunderstanding, or opposition?

4. Have you ever been asked to "check your faith at the door"? How did you—or how would you—respond to that challenge?

5. What "armor" do you put on each week to remain steadfast in your calling?

XIV

In God's Time
(From deferral to acceptance
into the Diaconate Formation)

"Create in me a clean heart, O God, and renew a steadfast spirit within me." — Psalm 51:10

The two years after my first Diaconate application felt longer than any I could remember. I continued serving as a lector and attending daily Mass, all the while waiting and praying for the next opportunity. When I finally reapplied, the interview began smoothly—until the panel asked if I still had an issue with whom I received the Eucharist. The question caught me off guard. I assured them I would receive from whoever was distributing the Eucharist at church and would have no problem with that. They seemed satisfied, but as I left, I couldn't help wondering if my response might still put my acceptance in question.

The interview was held in early spring, and we were told letters would arrive by late July or early August. When my letter came, I opened it to find the word I had been longing for: *accepted.* In hindsight, I can now see that God's delay the first time was not denial—it was preparation. If I had been in the earlier class, I would have struggled much more. In the class I entered, I met another candidate who faced challenges similar to mine. We supported each other through nearly every year of Diaconate training. Often, the best way to get through difficulties is to help someone else who is also struggling. I sometimes think neither of us could have made it without the other.

Whenever I came home with a passing exam grade, I would tell my wife, "I think we can do this." That first year—Aspirancy—was unlike anything I had ever experienced. They told us it "didn't really count as a year," which never made sense to me, because it felt like the most scrutinized year of all. We were watched closely. Every comment, every response, every moment in class was being quietly evaluated.

There were fifteen of us, and five men in my class received letters telling them they would not be continuing. Two of them I understood; they had openly spoken against the teachings of the Church during class. But the other three? I still don't know the reasons. Maybe it was the academic demands. Maybe it was something noticed in their discernment. Whatever the cause, it was a sobering reminder that none of us were guaranteed to remain in the program.

The academic load was heavier than anything I had expected. I prayed constantly just to keep my footing. Sometimes I would go to church, kneel before the tabernacle, and simply tell God, "If You want me in this, I need Your help to get through it."

One of the blessings of formation was having Angelo, a classmate who struggled even more than I did. Helping him helped me. Somehow, walking alongside someone else made the load feel lighter, and in turn, strengthened my resolve.

Looking back on those five years, I honestly see it as nothing short of miraculous that I made it through.

There were humbling moments, too, like the priest who once slammed my exam onto the desk and called it "heresy." His style of correction reminded me of my childhood, the feeling of getting knocked down just when I thought I was doing well. But instead of walking away, I kept going.

I also learned something important about the calling. If someone were to push through five years of this formation for ego or status, they would be out of their mind. The process is too demanding, too humbling, too exhausting to survive without a genuine call and a real love for the faith. That love—and that call—is what kept me moving forward, even on the days when I doubted everything about myself.

After the first year, each of us was assigned a spiritual director. I was blessed with Father Lawrence Bock from Holy Spirit Church in Newington, Connecticut—a man with the patience of a saint. He continually reassured me that I would make it through the formation process.

One of our training modules focused on near-death experiences. As I listened to others' stories of radical life changes, I couldn't help reflecting on my own transformation since October 21, 2006. My change had been so dramatic that it would have otherwise required intensive counseling, other interventions, or medication. But this was no midlife crisis or self-willed moral improvement—it was a divine intervention. I still wonder who may have been praying for my metanoia. I will find out one day. Ultimately, it was God who decided to bless me with such a beautiful gift, and I am grateful that I accepted it.

When I first heard Psalm 51, the Psalm of David, I felt an immediate connection. His plea for cleansing, renewal, and restoration mirrored my own experience:

"Have mercy on me, O God, according to your unfailing love; according to your great compassion blot out my transgressions. Wash away all my iniquity and cleanse me from my sin... Create in me a pure heart, O God, and renew a steadfast spirit within me... Restore to me the joy of your salvation and grant me a willing spirit, to sustain me... My sacrifice, O God, is a broken spirit; a broken and contrite heart you, God, will not despise."

Like David, I felt utterly cleansed, my soul made new. When God grants this kind of grace, the old, sinful behaviors lose their grip. Yet God does not erase our memories. My past remains in my mind, and when I recall it, I am appalled. That is the thorn in my flesh—just as Saint Paul described. While I sometimes wish those memories would vanish, they serve as a warning never to return to my former life.

In our near-death module, I also learned that many couples divorce after such transformative events. The change in one spouse can be so great that the other struggles to adapt. My wife, Barbara, admitted it took her over a year to believe the change in me was real. Before my metanoia, I never said "I love you." Now, I say it every time we part, hang up the phone, or simply walk through the door. That change is one of God's many gifts to me, along with Barbara herself—a blessing far beyond anything I deserve.

Looking back, I realize that the waiting, the setbacks, and the long formation years were never wasted. God was shaping me—not only for ordination but for a lifetime of ministry rooted in humility, gratitude, and love. My metanoia was not just a turning from sin, but a re-creation—God making me new and giving me the steadfast spirit I would need to serve Him faithfully.

Reflection Questions

1. When have you experienced God's "delay" in your life, and how did it ultimately prepare you for what came next?

2. Have you ever had to encourage or support someone who was going through a similar struggle? How did that shape your own journey?

3. How do you balance gratitude for God's cleansing grace with the humility of remembering your past?

4. Have you experienced a transformation that challenged the people closest to you? How did you walk through that season together?

5. What daily habits or words—like "I love you"—could become part of how you live out your renewed heart?

XV

When They Don't Believe (Finding peace when others doubt your conversion)

"If the world hates you, know that it has hated me before it hated you." — John 15:18

S ome family members and acquaintances still don't believe that what happened to me was divine intervention. At first, that hurt deeply. I couldn't understand why they couldn't see God's hand in my transformation. But then I remembered who I was before October 21, 2006—closed off, stubborn, and unwilling to change, no matter what anyone said. If I had resisted so completely, why should I expect others to believe or follow immediately?

There were times when I became upset that my closest loved ones had not returned to the faith after hearing my story. Not long after I was assigned to my current parish, a former colleague from the Hartford Police Department, someone who also happened to be a parishioner, posted on a Facebook group called *Hartford Police: Then and Now*. It's a page where past and present officers share memories, updates, and old stories. He wrote, "You won't believe this, look who's the deacon at my church."

The comments rolled in. Most were positive. Some were shocked. A few were the kind of disbelief that comes from knowing who I used to be: *You've got to be kidding me… wow.*

Oddly enough, I found it more humorous than hurtful. Maybe that was an old defense mechanism surfacing. Or maybe it was simply the fact that outside opinions don't cut as deeply anymore. If people who knew the old me struggle to believe the change, I can live with that.

Where the pain still finds its way in is much closer to home. It's one thing for former co-workers to doubt what God has done in my life. It's another when those I love most do not feel moved by it in their own faith. Every time this thought came, I stopped and thought of Jesus. I am not Jesus, but I can identify with Him in this way: not everyone believed Him, either. Who was I to expect a different outcome? If people could doubt the Son of God, why should I be surprised when they doubt me?

That realization didn't erase the pain. It still hurts when people I love remain distant from the Church. That reality hurts in a way I rarely speak about. But I find consolation in knowing I am in good company. Jesus Himself was doubted, rejected, and misunderstood.

I also find hope in His words to Saint Faustina:

"Let the weak, sinful soul fear not to approach Me, for even if it had more sins than there are grains of sand in the world, all would be drowned out in the immeasurable depths of My mercy."

My metanoia taught me something important—my role is not to force belief. My role is to live out the mercy and grace I've been given and to trust that God will work in His time, just as He did in mine.

Reflection Questions

1. Have you ever been discouraged when others didn't believe your testimony or spiritual experience? How did you respond?

2. How does remembering Jesus' own rejection change the way you view skepticism from others?

3. What does it look like for you to "live out" your faith without pressuring others to believe?

4. How can you trust God's timing in the faith journey of your loved ones?

5. What words of mercy—like Jesus' message to Saint Faustina—can you hold onto when you feel discouraged?

XVI

Through the Dark Night
(Lessons from silence, struggle,
and service)

"Be still, and know that I am God." — Psalm 46:10

In our formation years, a priest once spoke about the "Dark Night" experienced by great mystics and saints. I remember thinking that my love for God would keep me from ever facing such a thing. But God has a way of humbling us when we say "never."

During my seventh year after ordination, I began to feel a troubling separation from Him—a dryness in my prayer life that left me searching for what had changed. Over several months, I sensed something was wrong, but I couldn't quite name it. My relationship with God felt clouded, distant.

I thought about what a coach might tell a struggling team: "Go back to the basics and examine what's different now." When I took that advice to heart, I realized I had stopped attending Mass on days I wasn't serving as a deacon. I remembered one of our instructors saying, "After four or five Masses in one weekend, I'm all Massed out. No more church—I'm all churched out." I had thought at the time that I never wanted *to feel that way*. But now I could see how easy it was to slip.

So, I returned to the basics: attending Mass even when I wasn't assigned, receiving the Body of Christ as often as possible, and frequenting the Sacrament of Reconciliation.

The Silent Retreat

Annual retreats for deacons are required, but these were interrupted by COVID-19. I had long been intrigued by the idea of a silent retreat, and I found one at Enders Island in Mystic, Connecticut. You could choose total silence or occasional conversation with clergy; I chose complete silence, even during meals.

I made the reservation with anticipation, but as I drove closer, anxiety crept in. Seeing signs for the retreat center made me take a deep breath and steady myself. Two days and two nights lay ahead. As I entered the parking lot, butterflies filled my stomach. *That's it,* I thought, *silence begins now.*

I checked into my room and went to the dining hall. A nun, also on silent retreat, shared my table, but we did not speak. As much as I wanted to ask her advice or pose spiritual questions, that was not the nature of this retreat.

That first night, I spent hours in the chapel before the Blessed Mother. I brought a notepad and began writing everything I was feeling—fears, doubts, questions. I cried as I wrote, filling page after page. To this day, I haven't read those pages, but I know that four hours later, I felt lighter, unburdened. I had poured my heart out to God.

The next day, I prayed and walked the beautiful grounds. While the location was stunning, I knew the real work of a retreat comes from what you put into it. I could have broken my silence at any time—called my wife, made small talk—but I resisted. That choice became a deeper test than I expected.

Confession and Grace

Midway through the retreat, I sought out a priest and made a face-to-face confession. I wasn't embarrassed; I was ready. That moment refilled what I call my "grace tank." It felt like the night had lifted. The Sacrament of Reconciliation had renewed my peace.

Struggles don't disappear after confession, but they're a vital check-and-balance for the soul. Even minor lapses—a sharp word, a lack of kindness—can chip away at your relationship with God. The key is to notice, ask for grace, and make a change.

Formation Lessons

During formation, there were humbling moments. Once, Father returned an exam on Saint Paul's letters and announced to the whole class, "Mr. Blanchette, this test result is heresy." My score was thirty-five out of one hundred. Instead of getting angry, I worked harder.

My classmates included a corporate attorney and a multilingual teacher—both admitted that the diaconate was the hardest thing they had ever done. That honesty encouraged me. We coped through prayer, study, and laughter. In fact, we laughed so much that when the archbishop visited, he remarked, "I hear this class likes to laugh a lot." He was right—humor and prayer kept us going.

One instructor warned, "The biggest mistake after ordination is to stop learning." I had thought I'd learned enough, but I soon realized I was still learning every day—especially when preparing homilies.

Homiletics class brought its own humbling moment. After delivering my final homily, I silently congratulated myself, only to hear the priest say, "Mr. Blanchette, your voice puts me to sleep. You have a telephone voice that can put anyone to sleep." I laughed about it later, but it pushed me to work on my articulation with the help of my daughter, a speech-language pathologist. I began vocal exercises to speak more clearly and deliberately.

Living the Ongoing Metanoia

Returning to the basics—Mass, confession, silence—helped me find my footing again. That retreat reminded me that even in ministry, it's easy to drift from God in small ways. My metanoia didn't end the day I walked out of that basilica in Texas; it continues in every retreat, every confession, every challenge.

Formation taught me discipline, perseverance, and even how to laugh through difficulty. Most of all, it taught me to keep seeking God—and never to think I'm immune from the same struggles that humbled the saints before me.

Reflection Questions

1. Have you ever thought, *that will never happen to me,* only to experience exactly what you dismissed? How did God use it to teach you?

2. When your relationship with God feels distant, what "basics" help you reconnect?

3. How comfortable are you with silence in prayer or retreat? What might a period of intentional silence reveal in your heart?

4. What's your "grace tank," and how do you refill it?

5. How do you balance humility and perseverance when faced with criticism or failure?

6. In what ways do you continue learning about your faith after formal instruction or training has ended?

XVII

From Calling to Commission (Ordination, first sermons, and a future in service)

"I thank Christ Jesus our Lord, who has given me strength, that he considered me trustworthy, appointing me to his service." — 1 Timothy 1:12

In February 2016, the ten of us who remained were required to appear individually before a preaching board consisting of two priests and two deacons. The board would vote on whether we would be granted the faculties to preach. Not everyone knows this, but a man can be ordained a deacon without being given the faculties to preach.

Two weeks before ordination, while waiting to meet with the archbishop, I asked the Director of the Diaconate Formation when we would know if we had received those faculties. He asked, "Did you get a letter?" I said no. He smiled, replied, "You have nothing to worry about," and walked away. That was how I learned—months after the February board meeting—that I had been approved. I knew God had brought me this far for a reason.

When the time came to meet with the archbishop, I was more nervous than I expected. I had carried a quiet fear for months about sharing the truth of my calling, that it was the Blessed Mother who had led me back to the Church and into ministry. I worried that saying it out loud might sound strange or overly mystical, that it might raise a red flag or make me seem unbalanced. Everyone else had stories about a priest or a deacon approaching them, asking if they had ever considered the diaconate. No one had ever approached me. My invitation had come in a very different way.

But as I sat there with the archbishop, I felt moved to be completely honest. I told him what I believed: that the Blessed Mother had been the one who guided me here. When he responded with calm acceptance and told my wife they found me worthy of ordination, the relief washed over me. It was the confirmation I needed—of both my calling and God's hand in it.

Our wives were also present there because they have the final say in whether we are ordained. The archbishop told my wife, "We find your husband worthy to be ordained a deacon in the Catholic Church. Are you in agreement?" She answered, "Yes—on the condition he makes me spaghetti sauce every Sunday when he is finished at church." The archbishop laughed, turned to me, and asked if I agreed. "Absolutely," I said. And so every Sunday, unless my wife tells me otherwise, I make spaghetti sauce after Mass.

Vesting and Gratitude

The week leading up to ordination felt unlike anything I had experienced since childhood. The only way I can describe it is the feeling I used to have waiting for Christmas—pure excitement, anticipation, a joy so deep it almost felt electric. I hadn't felt that kind of happiness in years.

We were told to choose a clergy member to vest us at ordination. I requested the priest who had heard my confession in Texas, the very one God used to bring me back to the Catholic Church. He graciously agreed to come.

Two years earlier, at another ordination, I had seen two deacons choose two priests each to vest them. So I thought nothing of inviting the pastor from the church I attended before ordination as well. However, I later learned that only one clergy member can perform the vesting. Father Nadolny, my pastor, vested me, while Father Labus—understanding and gracious—was still present for the ceremony.

It meant the world to have the priest who first welcomed me home to the Church place the vestments on me that marked my new ministry.

On the day of ordination, after the ceremony, Father Labus pulled me aside and said, "I can see the elation on your face." He was right. For so long, smiling had not come naturally to me. Those who knew me during my earlier years would remember how rare it was to see me truly happy. But that day, something came back. The ordination restored my smile.

The Last Class and First Assignment

At our final class before ordination, one of my classmates reflected, "You know, we've been meeting here every Tuesday for the past five years, and tonight it ends." We would miss laughing together, though not necessarily the classes themselves. We had supported one another, become close, and made the familiar promise graduates often make—

that we would always stay in touch. Like many such promises, it lasted only for a short time.

On ordination day, we also learned where we would serve. I was assigned to Holy Spirit Parish in Newington, Connecticut—where my spiritual director from formation, Father Bock, was the pastor. This was a tremendous blessing. Not only was I already familiar with him, but I knew his mentorship would continue to shape me in my ministry as a deacon.

First Preaching Experiences

A week or two before ordination, I attended Mass at Sacred Heart Church in East Berlin, Connecticut. As I listened to the pastor's homily, I found myself wondering if I could ever preach as well—or preach at all—in front of so many people.

Yet the day after ordination, I delivered my first sermon at Sacred Heart. Preaching for the first time was a battle against every insecurity I had. My experience in the homiletics program had been rough. One of the priests who trained us was harsh and relentless, often tearing apart our attempts at writing or delivering a homily. His critiques felt less like feedback and more like the kind of mental battering I remembered from childhood. By the end of that year, my confidence in preaching was almost nonexistent.

So when I stepped up to preach my first homily, my voice trembled. I wasn't sure I could even get through it. But the parishioners at Sacred Heart, and later Holy Spirit and Annunciation, met me with kindness, not criticism. The parishioners were warm and gracious. They even clapped afterward—perhaps in relief that I had finished!

Some have since told me how far I've come. They'll say, "If you heard yourself back then, you wouldn't believe the difference now." I thank them every time. Their patience gave me room to grow. Their kindness helped me find my voice. Even today, when I step into the pulpit, I still feel a mix of nerves and excitement, but now it's the kind that fuels me rather than frightens me.

The first time I served at Mass at Holy Spirit, I was welcomed with the same warmth. I was still nervous when preaching, but parishioners reassured me with kind words and encouragement. Over the years—now at Annunciation Parish, after Holy Spirit merged with Saint Mary's—the priests and parishioners have continued to be supportive. They have given me room to grow every single week in the ministry of the diaconate, and for that I am deeply grateful.

Ongoing Growth in Ministry

Serving alongside my spiritual director, Father Bock, was an extraordinary gift. His guidance, along with the ongoing support of parishioners, has shaped me into the deacon I am today.

Ministry, I have learned, is not a destination. It is a lifelong journey of growth, humility, and service. As Saint Augustine said, "There is no saint without a past, no sinner without a future." My metanoia was not just the moment God called me back to the Church—it is the daily choice to serve Him with gratitude, to share His mercy with others, and to believe that no matter where you have been, His grace can make all things new.

Reflection Questions

1. Have you ever received encouragement that gave you peace about a major step in your faith or vocation? How did it affect your confidence?

2. In what ways have mentors, spiritual directors, or supportive friends shaped your journey of service?

3. How has God used moments of nervousness or uncertainty to reveal His presence in your calling?

4. What traditions, promises, or symbolic acts (like being vested) have deepened your sense of purpose in ministry or service?

5. How do you continue to grow in humility and skill after reaching a milestone in your spiritual or vocational life?

6. Reflect on Saint Augustine's words: "There is no saint without a past, no sinner without a future." How does this truth speak to your own journey?

XVIII

The Father I Feared, the Father I Found, and the Truth That Rewrote My Past

For most of my life, I carried a question that I never had the courage to ask. It started the day my sister died in a car accident in 1980, at the young age of 21. My parents were living in Wyoming at the time and flew back to Connecticut for the funeral. I heard later from my older sister that my father cried on the flight home. My mother looked at him and said, "What are you crying for? She wasn't even your kid."

At the time, I was a teenager, and the meaning did not sink in. Years later, it did. But even as an adult, even as a police officer, even as a homicide commander, I was still afraid to confront the man I called my father. He was a menacing presence my entire life, and that fear never really left.

My mother died young at fifty-seven. My father died a few years later at sixty-seven. I was close to forty, still on the police force, still holding those questions inside. When he died, something in me prompted me to look for answers.

I started by calling one of my aunts. Her response hit like a punch.

"Oh, you didn't know? The man who raised you wasn't your father."

She said it casually, as if she had been waiting to use the secret as a weapon. She had her reasons for being angry with me, so I took her words cautiously. But she gave me two names. I ran them both through the department's systems. The first name led nowhere. The second one stopped me cold: Tom Clinch.

I found his address. I drove there off duty. I waited outside his house until he pulled out of the driveway. He noticed me following and pulled over.

"Are you following me?" he asked.

"Yes," I said.

"Are you Tom Clinch?"

He nodded. I said the words I had held inside for decades: "From what I understand, I'm your son."

He started crying. He said, "I thought this day would never come."

My oldest sister and I took a genetic test. The results came back at 99.9 percent. We were his children. Every one of us was.

The truth unraveled quickly after that. When my mother was sixteen, she dated both Tom Clinch and James Blanchette, the man who raised me. My grandfather disliked Clinch. When Clinch got my mother pregnant, she convinced Blanchette that the baby was his, and he married her. She continued having children with Clinch while staying married to Blanchette. My siblings and I grew up thinking one man was our father, while another quietly lived in the background of our lives.

It was the kind of twist that could drop a person to their knees. What surprised me most was my reaction.

I did not feel betrayed. Instead, I felt grateful.

There is a kind of dark humor that develops in people who survive difficult homes. Maybe that is why the first thing I said to my wife was, "I guess I should be grateful the abusive father raised me, because at least he baptized me Catholic." It sounds strange, but it was true. My biological father was Episcopalian. If life had gone differently, I might not have been raised in the Catholic faith at all. The path that brought me to the diaconate might never have existed.

Life has a strange way of weaving itself together. Before I knew the truth, I once worked a road job where I met a gas company employee. I remember thinking, "This guy is one of the nicest men I've ever met." Years later, I learned he was my father.

And there was another twist. My wife grew up in the next town over. She went to school with one of my cousins—one of Clinch's nieces. I sometimes think about what would have happened if I had brought her home as a teenager, introducing her to my mother. My mother would have known immediately who she was. It is unsettling to consider how close I came to crossing paths with the truth without ever seeing it.

What I carry now is not resentment. It is understanding. My life could have gone in a thousand different directions.

Some of them would have been easier. Some far worse. But all of them would have led away from the path I am on today.

My father by blood did not raise me. My father by law did not love me well. But the life I lived—painful as parts of it were—shaped me into the man I became. And in a strange, almost accidental way, it kept me in the faith that would one day save me.

I can look back now and say this with clarity: I would not be who I am today if the truth had been different. And I can finally say it without fear.

Conclusion

Looking back, I can see that my journey to the diaconate was not defined by a single moment of calling, but by countless moments—some joyful, some humbling—that drew me closer to Christ. From the deep silence of Enders Island to the nervous energy of my first homily, from unexpected lessons in the "Dark Night" to the steady encouragement of parishioners, each experience has been another stone in the path God has laid before me.

Formation taught me more than theology or liturgy—it taught me that service requires humility, perseverance, and a willingness to keep learning long after the classes are over. It showed me that the grace to serve is renewed daily, not only in the sacraments but also in the quiet choices we make to return to the basics: prayer, confession, Eucharist, and a heart open to God's voice.

I have learned that ministry is not about being immune to struggle, but about being willing to walk through it with faith. It is about knowing that our past does not disqualify us and that our future is shaped not by our own strength, but by the grace of God who calls us. *"Be still, and know that I am God"* (Psalm 46:10) has become a steady reminder that His timing is perfect, even when the road feels uncertain.

And when doubt or discouragement crept in, I returned to the truth of 1 Timothy 1:12: *"I thank Christ Jesus our Lord, who has given me strength, that he considered me trustworthy, appointing me to his service."* Those words remind me that the One who calls also equips—and that His appointment is not based on my perfection, but on His mercy. My metanoia is ongoing—an ever-deepening "yes" to God's call, one homily, one confession, one Sunday spaghetti sauce at a time.

The road from that Basilica in Texas to the ambo at Annunciation Parish has been marked by grace upon grace. **I made my peace, and so can you.**

And if there is one truth my journey has made clear, it is this: the One who appoints us to His service also sustains us in it, from the first moment of our calling to the very last day we serve in His name.

"I am confident of this, that the One who began a good work in you will continue to complete it until the day of Christ Jesus." — Philippians 1:6

May this promise be the heartbeat of every servant of God—that the work He begins in us, He will bring to completion, until we see Him face to face.

Reflection Questions

1. When has God's timing or plan for you looked different from what you expected—and how did you respond in that moment?

2. What "basics" of faith might you need to return to in order to rekindle your relationship with God?

3. How can you say a deeper "yes" to God's call in your life right now, trusting Him to equip you for what lies ahead?

About The Author

The person I am today is nothing I would have ever imagined, nor did I plan it. I am a Deacon in the Archdiocese of Hartford, Connecticut, and I will be celebrating my 10th year as a Deacon on June 4, 2026. I have been assigned to Annunciation Parish since my ordination.

I was a member of the Hartford, CT Police Department and a Social Worker with the State of Connecticut, working with families. My ordination to the Diaconate was nothing that I ever planned for, nor had ever prepared for, nor did I ever expect in a million years to be ordained a Deacon. It was a divine calling, something I never thought was possible for anyone. However, I was completely wrong, and there is a true calling to the religious life.

My desire during my vocation is to have people realize that there is hope for them, no matter what their struggles are, no matter how impossible matters may be, or the situation that you might be in, that by turning yourself over to God, letting God take control of your entire life, will lead to them having peace in their lives.

Since my metanoia conversion, I have often said that I exchanged the .45 caliber Smith & Wesson semi-automatic firearm I carried for many years for the most powerful weapon that any person can carry, the rosary beads I now keep close at hand, a weapon of prayer for the spiritual battles of daily life.

Peace Deacon Jim

Reader Notes